THE

TOP TEN

MOST **LETHAL**
ANIMALS

whitestar·kids

LET'S BEGIN!

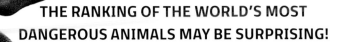

THE RANKING OF THE WORLD'S MOST DANGEROUS ANIMALS MAY BE SURPRISING!

What animal do you think is at the top of the list?
A shark, a lion, or maybe even a poisonous spider?
Are you sure?
Flip through the pages of this book to climb the
Top Ten and discover that even animals you'd
never expect can hide a lethal weapon!

IF YOU THINK YOU ALREADY KNOW EVERYTHING, KEEP READING. SURPRISES AWAIT— DANGEROUS ONES!

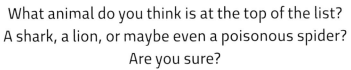

LETHAL WEAPON

TRIVIA

Look for these symbols to learn
unexpected **TRIVIA** and discover
what **LETHAL WEAPONS** make
these **TEN ANIMALS** worthy of
our ranking!

THE DANGER LEVEL WILL INCREASE AS WE COUNT DOWN FROM **TEN** ALL
THE WAY UP TO TERRIBLE NUMBER **ONE**!

At the bottom of the page you'll find the names of the **TEN ANIMALS** in our ranking. Try to guess each animal's position and write its name next to the number you think is correct. **AS YOU READ THE BOOK, YOU'LL FIND OUT HOW MANY YOU GUESSED RIGHT!**

1 _____

2 _____

Find out who I am by turning the page!

3 _____

4 _____

5 _____

6 _____

7 _____

8 _____

9 _____

10 _____

- GREAT WHITE SHARK
- HIPPOPOTAMUS
- POISON DART FROG

- HARPY EAGLE
- AFRICAN ELEPHANT
- MOSQUITO

- NILE CROCODILE
- TIGER
- POLAR BEAR
- PIRANHA

10 HARPY EAGLE

Even saying my name is scary!

SCIENTIFIC NAME:
Harpia harpyja

WINGSPAN: 6.5 ft (2 m)

This predator descends suddenly from the forest canopy to strike its prey; sloths, monkeys, and iguanas have no chance once they're in the grip of its **LONG TALONS**.

When hunting, this eagle lowers and moves its head feathers to direct **SOUND WAVES** toward its ears. That way, it can hear even the smallest noise. Plus, its vision is **8 TIMES BETTER THAN OURS**.

It eats nearly 2.2 lbs (1 kg) of meat a day and hides larger prey among tree branches, consuming its catch over several days.

WEIGHT:
13-20 lbs (6-9 kg) (females) / 9-11 lbs (4-5 kg) (males)

lbs

DIET:
carnivore
(eats other animals)

HABITAT:
the rain forests of South America

And just think, I'm only number 10!

LETHAL WEAPON
Talons over 4 in (10 cm) long. That's as long as a grizzly bear's!

TRIVIA
It builds huge nests, up to 5 ft (1.5 m) wide, which are used for years.

9

AFRICAN ELEPHANT

SCIENTIFIC NAME:
Loxodonta africana

HEIGHT: 9.5 ft (3 m)

Elephants are gentle giants, but like most animals, if disturbed or provoked, they can be surprisingly **AGGRESSIVE** and may even **VIOLENTLY CHARGE** who-ever is threatening them. With power-ful, **IMMENSE BODIES**, elephants can run at speeds exceeding **25 MILES (40 KM) PER HOUR**, overwhelming and trampling everything in their path.

TUSKS and **TRUNKS** are used to hurl whatever they wish in the air, flinging it far away with ease.

WEIGHT:
265 lbs (120 kg) (infants), 6.6 tons (6,000 kg) (adults)

DIET:
herbivore
(eats plants)

HABITAT:
African savannas

You don't want to bother me—I'm very fast!

LETHAL WEAPON
A mighty body, long tusks, and a muscular trunk.

TRIVIA
Its trunk is moved by 40,000 muscles!

7

TIGER

Whaaat?!
I thought I'd be
higher on the list!

SCIENTIFIC NAME:
Panthera tigris

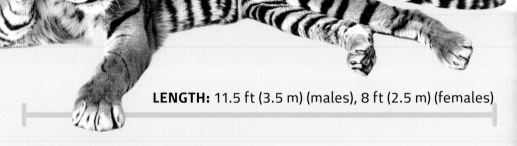

LENGTH: 11.5 ft (3.5 m) (males), 8 ft (2.5 m) (females)

Tigers have features that make them ferocious hunters: **CLAWS AS SHARP AS RAZORS**, **POINTED TEETH,** and **AGILITY**. In addition to these deadly weapons, which all **FELINES** have, tigers also have powerful **MUSCLES** and a robust body, making them the **BIGGEST** of all cats.

Tigers also have an unmistakable **STRIPED COAT** that allows them to blend in with the light and shadows created by vegetation, where they wait in **AMBUSH** for their prey.

 WEIGHT:
660 lbs (300 kg) (males), 400 lbs (180 kg) (females)

 DIET:
carnivore
(eats other animals)

 HABITAT:
forests

LETHAL WEAPON
Sharp claws and long, pointed canines!

TRIVIA
Tigers can eat up to 90 lbs (40 kg) of meat per meal

FEARSOME FELINES

All felines are similar to house cats, both in appearance and behavior. They have razor-like claws, sharp canines, large eyes, and straight ears. They hiss if they're frightened or angry; they're extremely agile and move silently. Their acrobatic prowess means their prey almost never stands a chance.

THESE THREE BIG CATS ARE AMONG THE MOST DANGEROUS BECAUSE THEY HAVE EXTREMELY LETHAL HUNTING TECHNIQUES.

Cheetah

CHEETAHS have perfected a strategy all their own: Unlike other felines, which surprise their prey, cheetahs pick individual prey out from a pack and then isolate the animal from the others. They then capture it using their impressive **SPEED**.

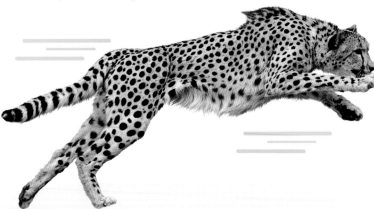

Super speed!

They go from zero to 60 mph (96 kph) in three seconds.

Lion

Felines are normally solitary animals, but **LIONS** are an exception, living in family groups consisting of **MULTIPLE FEMALES** and a smaller number of males. The group, called a pride, hunts together, with excellent results.

The power of a herd!

They are the only felines capable of killing prey much larger than themselves.

Jaguar

The spots on their fur help **JAGUARS** hide in the dappled shade of trees in South American jungles while they wait **SILENTLY** for their prey.

They're so good at hiding they seem invisible.

If born with black fur, jaguars and other wild cats are called **PANTHERS**.

PIRANHA

SCIENTIFIC NAME:
Pygocentrus natterei

LENGTH: up to 19.5 in (50 cm)

Piranhas have tiny teeth measuring just 1/8 of an inch (4 mm), but those teeth are as sharp as **RAZORS** and capable of cutting through any material, thanks in part to the **POWER OF THEIR JAWS**.

That's not all! Piranhas live in groups consisting of **HUNDREDS OF INDIVIDUALS**, so you can imagine how in a few minutes animals as large as capybaras can be ripped to **PIECES** and devoured in small bites. However, piranhas rarely attack live or healthy prey.

 WEIGHT:
8.6 lbs (3.9 kg)

 DIET:
carnivore
(eats other animals)

 HABITAT:
bodies of fresh water
in South America

I'm scarier when my friends are with me!

LETHAL WEAPON
Aggressiveness and lots of sharp little teeth.

TRIVIA
Within the group, there's always a dominant fish.

STRENGTH IN PACKS

Hunting with your peers certainly has its advantages: Joining forces let you capture even very large prey and ensure everyone gets a meal. However, you need to have a strategy, such as surrounding your prey and pushing it toward your comrades, who are waiting to ambush it. Within the group, there is usually one individual who coordinates the pack and directs each step of the attack.

IN ADDITION TO MAKING EACH HUNT MORE SUCCESSFUL, THE HERD PROTECTS BOTH ADULTS AND PUPS FROM BEING ATTACKED BY OTHER PREDATORS.

Wolf

WOLVES are fast, aggressive animals. They establish their own territory within which the herd hunts for food. They are led by an elderly and experienced couple: the alpha male and the alpha female.

Cunning and collaboration.

Wolves howl to rally the herd as they hunt.

Chimpanzee

The diet of **CHIMPANZEES** is based mainly on fruits and vegetables, but sometimes they feel the need to hunt: Adult males coordinate with each other to close off the escape routes of their prey, which is then captured by the group, who will share the spoils.

Intelligence and collaboration.

It takes many years— at least 10—for young chimps to learn their hunting techniques.

Hyena

The hunting technique of **HYENAS** consists of chasing prey to the point of exhaustion and then pouncing on the tired animal all at once. With their powerful teeth, they leave very few leftovers.

Teeth and collaboration.

Their bite is so powerful that it can shatter bones 2.4 in (6 cm) in diameter.

POISON DART FROG

SCIENTIFIC NAME:
Phyllobates terribilis

We're colorful...
and venomous!
LOOK OUT!

LENGTH: 1.8 in (4.5 cm)

This small animal is **TOXIC**, capable of poisoning 10 humans.

But only those who bite or eat this frog are in danger, however, because the poison is all stored in its skin. In fact, this frog uses its toxins only for defense: Its **BRILLIANT COLORS** notify predators of how dangerous it is, warning them to stay away! It's called the poison dart frog because Native peoples would rub the **ARROWHEADS** they used for hunting on the frogs' skin.

WEIGHT:
less than 1 oz
(30 g)

DIET:
insectivore
(eats insects)

HABITAT:
the rain forests
of South America

LETHAL WEAPON
Poisonous skin.

TRIVIA
The toxin comes from the insects it eats. When raised in captivity, this species of frog isn't poisonous!

VENOM ON LAND...

Venom is a secret weapon that many animals use to obtain a meal or to defend themselves. There are various types of poison; some cause only pain, some can disrupt the proper functioning of the nervous system, and some cause death.

ANIMALS HAVE SPECIAL GLANDS FOR PRODUCING VENOM. THEY OFTEN DELIVER IT TO THEIR VICTIMS' BODIES VIA SOMETHING SHARP, SUCH AS TEETH, STINGERS, OR QUILLS.

Insects

BEES, **WASPS**, and **HORNETS** (such as the Asian giant hornet) inject a toxic substance with their stinger, which, in addition to making the injured part swell, can cause a lethal allergic reaction.

Stingers.

Bees die after stinging.

Snakes

To inject their venom, **SNAKES** have special fangs that work sort of like needles. Taipans and black mambas are among the most dangerous snakes in the world; just two drops of their venom can stop an adult's heart and lungs from functioning.

Fangs.

Boas and pythons, on the other hand, are dangerous because of the force with which they crush their victims.

Spiders

In **SPIDERS**, venom is mainly used to liquefy the insides of their prey—that way it can be sucked out like a milkshake! Armed spider and black widow spider bites can also be deadly to humans.

A venomous bite.

Their webs are nets for trapping prey.

Platypus

Who would have guessed it? Cute **PLATYPUSES** defend themselves with venomous kicks, powerful enough to paralyze and kill smaller animals.

Spurs on their hind legs.

Only the males have spurs connected to venom glands.

19

...AND AT SEA!

Land creatures aren't the only ones to have powerful venom. There are lots of poisonous animals in the seas and oceans, more than you'd imagine! Jellyfish, cuttlefish, octopuses, and corals, as well as sea snakes and more than 1,200 species of fish, rely on toxins to win the daily struggle to survive.

TO DEFEND THEMSELVES, SOME ANIMALS INJECT THEIR VENOM, WHILE OTHERS STORE TOXINS WITHIN THEIR BODY TO POISON POTENTIAL PREDATORS.

Blue-ringed octopus

Despite its small size (no larger than a Ping-Pong ball), the graceful **BLUE-RINGED OCTOPUS** has a devastating bite: Its venom kills within minutes. Fortunately, they're quite rare.

Bite.

Iridescent blue rings appear on its body when it feels threatened and is ready to attack.

Pufferfish

The seas of Japan are home to the **FUGU**, a type of pufferfish whose flesh hides a very potent toxin, more poisonous than cyanide.
BE CAREFUL NOT TO EAT IT!

Poisonous flesh.

In Japan it's a delicacy, but it can only be prepared by super-specialized chefs.

Jellyfish

A jellyfish sting is not only painful, it can sometimes be deadly! The **BOX JELLYFISH** is a killer that roams the tropical seas; its tentacles are vehicles for one of the world's most powerful poisons.

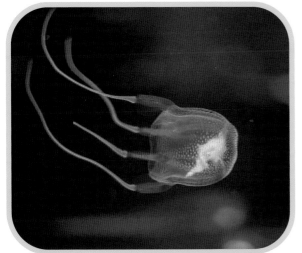

Stinging tentacles with more than 5,000 poison cells.

They're also called "sea wasps."

NILE CROCODILE

SCIENTIFIC NAME:
Crocodylus niloticus

LENGTH: up to 19.5 ft (6 m)

This large reptile is especially dangerous thanks to its **ABILITY TO HIDE** among aquatic vegetation.
Crocodiles are experts at staying **SUBMERGED** underwater for hours, totally motionless, waiting for unsuspecting prey to come along. Then, with surprising agility, they launch their attack, charging with their large mouth wide open, armed with **SHARP TEETH**. With the force of their deadly **JAWS**, they hold their prey underwater until it drowns.

WEIGHT:
1,540 lbs (700 kg)

DIET:
carnivore
(eats other animals)

HABITAT:
rivers and lakes
in Africa

LETHAL WEAPON
Powerful jaws and
sharp teeth.

TRIVIA
Their jaws are 5 times stronger
than a lion's!

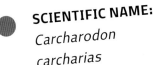

4 GREAT WHITE SHARK

SCIENTIFIC NAME:
Carcharodon carcharias

LENGTH: 19.5 ft (6 m) (females), 13 ft (4 m) (males)

The mouths of great white sharks are lined by **TRIANGULAR TEETH**, with an extra-sharp serrated edge. These teeth are continuously **REPLACED**.

Like the claws of a cat, shark teeth are retracted and only come out when the animal is ready to bite; it raises its jaw and the first row of teeth moves forward.

Thanks to their **POWERFUL SENSE OF SMELL**, great white sharks can detect their prey even from far away. The attack then occurs suddenly and usually from below.

WEIGHT:
1.7 tons (1,500 kg)

DIET:
carnivore
(eats other animals)

HABITAT:
seas and oceans

How can anyone be more dangerous than me?

LETHAL WEAPON
Bite and sense of smell.

TRIVIA
Sometimes before killing their prey, they "taste" it to see if it's edible.

LIKE SHARKS, BUT NICER!

Sharks are fish that have a skeleton made of cartilage and not bone, and they do not have scales to cover their skin. They are all carnivores, but not all are predators!

THERE ARE SHARKS THAT DO NOT FEED BY TEARING OTHER ANIMALS APART, BUT INSTEAD FILTER SMALL AQUATIC ORGANISMS THROUGH THEIR GILLS.

Whale shark

At 33 ft (10 m) long, whale sharks are the largest of all sharks, but they are often approached by divers because they don't attack or bite. They swim slowly, filtering 1,585 gallons (6,000 l) of water per hour with their wide mouth to collect plankton.

None!

It's believed that they can live up to 100 years!

Manta ray

The manta ray is a close relative of the shark but differs from them in its flattened body. Despite their somewhat "devilish" appearance, manta rays aren't aggressive or dangerous at all! Similar to whale sharks, they feed only on tiny plankton and other organisms that they gather by using their mouth like a net.

None!

Their pectoral fins resemble two wings that can reach 23 ft (7 m) when open!

POLAR BEAR

SCIENTIFIC NAME:
Ursus maritimus

Polar bears are the largest land-dwelling carnivores!

LENGTH: 10 ft (3 m)

The largest carnivores on land, polar bears spend half their day searching for prey.

Hunting takes place via **AMBUSH**: The polar bear waits patiently for a fat seal to come up to breathe from a hole in the ice. It then harpoons the seal with its **MIGHTY CLAWS** and drags it across the ice to devour it. A polar bear can eat up to 4.4 lbs (2 kg) of fat per day.

That **FAT** is needed to withstand very low temperatures.

WEIGHT:
1,500 lbs (680 kg)

DIET:
carnivore
(eats other animals)

HABITAT:
arctic ice

LETHAL WEAPON

Sharp teeth and large
paws with claws.

TRIVIA

Sniffs out prey more than
10 miles (15 km) away.

FURRY...BUT NOT TOO CUDDLY

Teddy bears are the playmates of many children, but real bears don't make very good pets. Indeed, they are the dominant predators in their habitat thanks to their strength, cleverness, advanced sense of smell and, of course, their mighty, sharp claws.

BUT NOT ALL BEARS ARE AGGRESSIVE AND SCARY. HOW DANGEROUS THEY ARE DEPENDS ON THEIR SIZE AND THEIR TASTE IN FOOD. HERE ARE THREE EXAMPLES: TWO DANGEROUS, ONE DEFINITELY NOT!

Grizzly bear

GRIZZLY BEARS have a mouth that can open almost 1 ft wide (30 cm) and canines that are as long as a finger! They also bite with enough force to crush a bowling ball. They like to roll around in anything that's rotting to hide their smell when they go hunting.

Powerful jaws.

They are mainly active at dusk and at night.

Sun bear

Although the baby of the "family," sun bears are very robust and often attack without reason. They have sharp teeth and huge paws with curved claws, which they usually use to open beehives and steal the honey inside.

Teeth and claws.

They are called sun bears because of the patch of light-colored hair on their chest.

Giant Panda

Although technically a bear, pandas don't share the same diet as their kin.
They spend 12 hours a day munching on bamboo leaves, devouring up to 33 lbs (15 kg).

None!

They have an extra finger to better grasp tree branches.

HIPPOPOTAMUS

SCIENTIFIC NAME:
Hippopotamus amphibius

Don't try to cuddle us!

LENGTH: up to 16.5 ft (5 m)

Don't be deceived by the calm, sweet appearance of this giant animal. Hippopotamuses are in fact tremendously **AGGRESSIVE** and dangerous! If irritated, they won't hesitate to forcefully charge at those who are annoying them. With their mouth wide open, they **BITE** really hard, so hard that it's often lethal because of their long fangs. Their massive body is also dangerous. Charging hard and **FASTER** than you'd think, hippos can overtake and crush anyone in their path.

WEIGHT:
3,000 lbs (1,400 kg) (females), up to 9,920 lbs (4,500 kg) (males)

DIET:
omnivore
(eats plants and animals)

HABITAT: rivers and lakes in Africa

LETHAL WEAPON

A big mouth armed
with long fangs.

TRIVIA

Hippos can run as fast
as 30 mph (50 kph)!

1

MOSQUITO

SCIENTIFIC NAME:
Anopheles sp.

Surprise! Never underestimate little creatures! We're the deadliest of all!

LENGTH: 0.25 in (5.5 mm)   **WINGSPAN:** 0.18 in (4.5 mm)

Although tiny, this insect is one of the most common causes of death among humans.

Deadly mosquitoes are widespread mainly in tropical regions, and their bite transmits **SERIOUS DISEASES**. By pricking the skin to draw blood, mosquitoes unintentionally inject humans with a microorganism, *Plasmodium falciparum*, that causes **MALARIA**, a deadly disease if not promptly treated.

lbs **WEIGHT:**
about 2 mg

DIET:
herbivore/sanguivore (the males feed on nectar, the females on blood)

 HABITAT:
stagnant water

LETHAL WEAPON

A stinger-like mouth.

TRIVIA

They can drink up to three times their weight in blood.

WILD QUESTIONS

10 QUESTIONS FOR 10 ANIMALS! IF YOU DON'T KNOW THE ANSWERS, THAT'S OK! GIVE THEM A TRY ANYWAY, AND DON'T WORRY ABOUT BEING RIGHT OR WRONG. THEN TURN THE PAGE TO SEE IF YOU GOT THEM RIGHT!

10- BESIDES ITS DEADLY CLAWS, WHAT CHARACTERIZES THE **HARPY EAGLE**?

A Speed

B Cunning

C Strength

9- WHAT ARE **ELEPHANT** TUSKS MADE OF?

A Ivory

B Bone

C Wood

8- WHERE DO **TIGERS** LIVE?

A African savannas

B Asian forests

C The jungles of South America

7- IF THE PREY IS A FISH, WHICH BODY PART DO **PIRANHAS** ATTACK FIRST?

A The belly

B The tail

C The dorsal fin

6- HOW LONG DOES THE EFFECT OF THE POISON DART FROG'S VENOM LAST?

A Years

B Weeks

C Hours

5- HOW MANY EGGS DOES A FEMALE **CROCODILE LAY**?

A 2-10

B 15-20

C 25-80

4- WHY DO **GREAT WHITE SHARKS** ATTACK PEOPLE?

A Because they're vicious assassins

B Because humans taste good

C Because they get confused

3- WHAT COLOR IS THE SKIN OF **POLAR BEARS**?

A Yellow

B Black

C Pink

2- WHY DO **HIPPOS** LEAVE THE WATER EVERY NIGHT?

A To look for a safe place to sleep

B To graze

C To save themselves from crocodiles

1- WHY DO ONLY FEMALE **MOSQUITOES** SUCK BLOOD?

A To nourish their eggs

B Because they're bigger

C Because that way they'll grow faster

WILD ANSWERS

10, C
Females, which are larger than males, can grab animals weighing up to 22 lbs (10 kg) in flight, carrying them directly to high tree branches without ever landing.

9, A
Made of ivory, tusks are the upper incisors of elephants. They appear at the age of two and grow throughout their lives (about 70 years). Unfortunately, poachers often kill elephants for their tusks, which are then sold illegally.

8, B
Tigers are found only on the Asian continent. They generally prefer to live in forests.
Their habitat is getting smaller and smaller, and unfortunately they are at risk of going extinct.

7, B
Once piranhas reach their prey, they bite at the eyes and especially the tail. In this way, the victim is immobilized and has no way to escape.

6, A Stored in the skin, the poison doesn't easily deteriorate, meaning it's maintained for a long time. Arrowheads rubbed in these toxins can retain their deadly qualities for more than two years.

5, C Up to 80 eggs can be laid at a time, inside nests dug in the sand along river banks. Mother crocodiles are very protective of their nests, and once the babies are born, she brings them with her into the water, carrying them gently in her mouth.

4, C Attacks on humans by great white sharks are generally due to inexperience. The silhouette of a surfboard or a person swimming is mistaken for that of a seal or other prey. After all, sharks don't have great vision!

3, B Polar bears have black skin because this color better absorbs all the heat from the sun's rays through its thick fur, which is made up of hairs that look white but are actually transparent.

2, B Given their size, hippos devour a very large amount of grass. They graze more than 77 lbs (35 kg) of it every night, traveling as far as 6 miles (10 km) to reach the places where it's most abundant. It was recently discovered that hippos occasionally eat dead animals as well.

1, A Male mosquitoes only eat flower nectar and plant sap. Females, on the other hand, bite and drink blood when they need to lay eggs because blood contains useful nutrients, such as iron and protein, necessary for their eggs to mature.

CRISTINA BANFI

With a degree in natural sciences from the University of Milan, Cristina Banfi has taught at several schools. She has been involved in science communication and education for more than 20 years and has been part of publishing projects in both scholastic and popular fields, particularly for children and young people.
In recent years, she has written several books for White Star.

PHOTO CREDITS

All photographs are from Shutterstock except the following:
Getty Images p. 2 bottom left, p. 3 bottom center, p. 16 top left, p. 19 bottom, and pp. 27, 29, 37 top.

WS whitestar kids™ is a trademark of White Star s.r.l.

© 2023 White Star s.r.l.
Piazzale Luigi Cadorna, 6 - 20123 Milan, Italy
www.whitestar.it

Translation: Katherine Kirby
Editing: Michele Suchomel-Casey

Second printing, January 2024

ISBN 978-88-544-1993-3
  2 3 4 5 6   28 27 26 25 24

Printed and manufactured in Türkiye by Bilnet Matbaacılık ve Yayıncılık A.Ş Ümraniye/İSTANBUL

MIX
Paper from responsible sources
FSC® C178000

Editorial Coordination
Giada Francia

Graphic design and layout
Valentina Figus